The Church Is All of You

Thoughts of Archbishop Oscar Romero

Compiled and translated
by James R. Brockman, S.J.

WINSTON PRESS

242
R

Library of Congress Catalog Card Number: 83-51389

ISBN: 0-86683-838-4

Printed in the United States of America

5   4   3   2   1

Winston Press, Inc.
430 Oak Grove
Minneapolis, Minnesota 55403

"God's best microphone is Christ, and Christ's best microphone is the church, and the church is all of you."

Oscar A. Romero
January 27, 1980

Preface

Archbishop Oscar A. Romero gave his life, in the words of Pope John Paul II, "for the church and the people of his beloved country" of El Salvador. His death from an assassin's bullet on March 24, 1980, crowned a life of service as priest and bishop. During his three years as archbishop of San Salvador, he became known across the world as a fearless defender of the poor and the suffering. The universities of Georgetown and Louvain gave him honorary degrees, and British parliamentarians nominated him for the Nobel Prize for Peace. Yet he earned also the hatred and calumny of powerful persons in his own country—hatred that inevitably led to his martyrdom.

Week after week for three years, Archbishop Romero's voice rang out over El Salvador, crying out against murder and torture, exhorting his people to seek peace and forgiveness and to build a more just society. By means of the archdiocese's radio station (unless its transmissions were jammed or its plant too badly damaged from dynamite blasts) he kept a whole nation hanging on his words. It seemed that one could hardly help hearing his voice from some radio on Sunday morning, especially in the neighborhoods of the poor and in the villages of the peasants. Oscar Romero achieved his rare eloquence not by writing polished sermons but by speaking directly to his listeners about their lives, and especially about the lives of the poor, whose sufferings, he said, "touch the very heart of God." The majority of Salvadorans are poor. It was mostly the poor who filled the cathedral for his 8 A.M. Sunday Mass, and it was the poor who surrounded him on his visits to even the most isolated hamlets of his diocese. But persons of all kinds testified that he and his words strengthened their faith, and he in turn found his own faith reinforced by the people.

This selection of Archbishop Romero's thoughts is meant to enable others to know this man of faith and to experience the power of his words.

Translator's note: The selections of Archbishop Romero's words are taken from his homilies, except where noted otherwise. When I thought the reader might be helped by looking up the entire Bible passage on which Archbishop Romero was preaching, or the readings of the Mass he was celebrating, I have given the Bible references. Translations of Bible texts used in this book are my own, though I am indebted to certain traditional renderings.

Contents

Foreword

I just finished reading the collection of quotations from Archbishop Romero that James Brockman has so ably brought together in this book. As I was reading I felt as if his spirit was drawing me closer and closer to the truth, that is, the true relationship with God. When I finally reached his last words, a deep silence came over me and I realised that something new had happened to me.

It is not easy to give words to this spiritual event that took place during the reading of Oscar Romero's unpretentious, unadorned, and unambiguous words. Maybe the best way to summarise what happened to me is to say that I had encountered a man of God marked by humility and confidence, calling me to conversion and action. In this foreword I want to express more fully the meaning of this encounter. Thus I hope to offer a spiritual place in which a similar encounter can take place for the many who will read this book.

Oscar Romero is a humble man of God. His humility pervades all he says. That probably is the main reason why it was possible for me to read these very challenging and demanding words. They are spoken by someone who is very close to me. Oscar Romero does not speak from a distance. He does not hide his fears, his brokenness, his hesitations. There is a warmth in his words that opens my heart to listen. It is as if he puts his arm around my shoulder and slowly walks with me. He shares with me his struggles: "God knows how hard it was for me to become archbishop. How timid I have felt before you. . . ." He explains to me who he wants to be for his people: "The attitude to be taken . . . is not 'I am in charge here!' . . . You are only a human being. . . . You must . . . serve the people according to God's will and not according to your whim." He does not want to be different: "The shepherd does not want security while they give no security to his flock." He is aware that he receives as much as he gives: "Precisely in those charisms that the Holy Spirit gives to his people the bishop finds the touchstone of his authenticity." "With this people it is not hard to be a good shepherd. They are a people that impel to their service. . . ." He asks for forgiveness and prayer: "I beg pardon for not having shown all the fortitude the gospel asks. . . ." "I ask your prayers to be faithful—that I will not abandon my people but that together with them I will run all the risks that my ministry demands." As I hear him speak to me in this way, I know that he is indeed the good shepherd who lays down his life for his friends. He lays down for me his own broken humanity, his fears, his sins, his hopes, and thus opens my heart to listen to his words of faith.

Oscar Romero's humility is the fruitful ground of his confidence. He is a man "con fide," with trust, an unlimited trust in Jesus Christ. As I listen to him I realise that I am listening to a man who has fixed his eyes on Jesus and thus can walk safely amidst the pain and suffering of his people. In the midst of despair he calls for hope: "The more full of troubles and problems we are, the more bewildering life's ways, the more we must look up to the skies and hear the good news: 'A savior is born to you.'" In the midst of powerlessness he offers courage: "Let us not be disheartened as though human realities made impossible the accomplishment of God's plans." In the midst of agony he announces the resurrection: "Those who have disappeared will reappear. . . . Affliction . . . will become Easter joy if we join ourselves to Christ. . . ." In the midst of violence he preaches the beatitudes: "There are people who opt for guerrilla war, for revolution. . . . The church's option is for the beatitudes. . . . Christ was sowing a moral revolution in which we human beings come to change ourselves from worldly thinking." In the midst of hatred he proclaims love: "I wish to show that the nucleus of my life is to witness the love of God to humans and of humans among themselves. . . . I have tried to follow the supreme shepherd, Jesus Christ, who directed his love to all." His confidence is so strong that he can say without any ambiguity: "I simply want to be the builder of a great affirmation, the affirmation of God, who loves us and who wants to save us." As I let the words of Archbishop Romero enter more deeply into my heart I gradually come to experience that this humble but confident man becomes also for me the great affirmation of God's inexhaustible love.

Let me now speak about the other side of this encounter. It is my side! How can I respond when a voice, so humble but so strong, touches me deeply? This book tells me clearly to what Oscar Romero invites me. His words are a clear call to conversion and action. When Archbishop Oscar Romero first spoke the words gathered in this book, he directed himself to all the people in El Salvador, people from the left as well as people from the right, people supportive of the guerrillas as well as people in the government and the army, people who were being killed as well as their killers, the oppressed as well as the oppressors. But now after these words have been sanctified by his martyrdom they have become words for all people, and especially for the people of the United States. Now they have become words asking for a response not only from the people in El Salvador but also from us, who participate, willingly or unwillingly, knowingly or unknowingly, in the violence and destruction suffered by the Salvadorans. And who are we? Whether we want it or not, we are the rich, the powerful, the oppressors who pay the bills for the arms that kill and torture in El Salvador. And thus Oscar Romero's words become a call to conversion. He says it loudly: "I call to everyone: Let us be converted so that Christ may look upon our faith and have mercy on us." To me, a Christian of the first world, he says without hesitation: "When one knows that financial capital, political influence, and power are worthless, . . . that is when one begins to experience faith and conversion." To me, the rich Christian, he says: "When we speak of the church of the poor, we are simply telling the rich also: Turn your eyes to this church and concern yourselves for the poor as for yourselves." It is painful to hear these words as directed to myself, but since they come from a man as faithful as Oscar Romero, I may be able to let them come close and lead me to repentance and conversion. I am not an outsider to El Salvador's agony. I participate in it by continuing to adore the idols of "money, political interest, and national security" and by not letting the God of Jesus Christ, who became poor for my sake, guide all of my life and all of my actions. Thus I am called to confess my role in the violence that Oscar Romero condemns, to ask for forgiveness for my sins against the people who are exploited and oppressed, and to be converted.

But Oscar Romero asks for more. He asks for action that leads to justice and peace. One of the dominant themes of his sermons is the incarnation: Christ is the Word that became flesh in history. Conversion leads to engagement: "Some want to keep a gospel so disembodied that it doesn't get involved at all in the world it must save. Christ is now in history. Christ is in the womb of the people. Christ is now bringing about the new heavens and the new earth." He leaves little doubt that a true Christian must participate in the work of liberation: "Christ appeared . . . with the signs of liberation: shaking off oppressive yokes, bringing joy to hearts, sowing hope. And this is what God is doing now in history." Again and again Oscar Romero stresses the active nature of God's word. "We cannot separate God's word from the historical reality in which it is proclaimed. . . . It is God's word because it enlightens, contrasts, repudiates, praises what is going on today in this society." A commitment to the word requires a commitment to history. Such a commitment challenges us to recognise, criticise, and change the unjust structures of a society that causes suffering. Such a commitment leads to conflicts and persecutions. Such a commitment can even ask of us that we give everything, even our life, for the cause of justice and peace. Archbishop Romero calls to the hard service of the word. "What marks the genuine church is when the word, burning like the word of the prophets, proclaims to the people and denounces: proclaims God's wonders to be believed and venerated, and denounces the sins of those who oppose God's reign, so that they may tear those sins out of their hearts, out of their societies, out of their laws—out of the structures that oppress, that imprison, that violate the rights of God and of humanity. This is the hard service of the word." To this active service I feel called by Oscar Romero, the martyr of El Salvador. It is indeed a very great demand, but it is the demand of Jesus himself, re-spoken in the concrete historical context in which we live. As a Christian I am invited—yes, required—to work with all my energy for the salvation of the world. Oscar Romero makes it clear that such a work cannot be spiritualised: "All practices that disagree with the gospel must be removed if we are to save people. We must save not the soul at the hour of death but the person living in history." Thus conversion opens me to action, an action for justice and peace in the concreteness of our contemporary society.

The encounter with Oscar Romero, the humble but confident man of God calling me to conversion and action for peace and justice, was the fruit of the texts this book contains. I never met Archbishop Romero during his life. But I met him in a very special way in his words, which truly became flesh not only through the way he lived but also through the way he died. His life and death have given these words a unique authority. It is the authority of the compassionate shepherd, the shepherd who suffers with his people and gives his life for them. One day Oscar Romero said to his people: "I sense that there is something new in the archdiocese. I am a man, frail and limited, and I do not know what is happening, but I do know that God knows." This spiritual intuition proved to be true. Something very new is happening in the church of Central America. Out of the anguish and agony of his people the Spirit of God is fashioning a new creation. I pray that those who will read this book and allow the words of Oscar Romero to enter into their innermost being will also sense that something new is happening in them.

Henri J. M. Nouwen

1977

Baptism made us one body with Christ,
and in Christ we are one with him
and cannot betray all that flows from that:
the new human being.
It is a new being with a heart cleansed of all sin,
a new person who does not speak with animosity
in the heart,
who never furthers violence, hatred, rancor.
It is one who loves as the heart of Christ loves.

June 19, 1977

Note: Oscar Romero became archbishop of San Salvador on February 22, 1977, after several priests had been expelled from the country and while the church of the archdiocese was under attack in the media. On March 12, the pastor of the rural parish of Aguilares was ambushed and assassinated, along with two parishioners. In May, military forces raided the town, killed dozens of people, desecrated the church and the Eucharist, and deported the three remaining priests. The archbishop was not allowed to visit the parish, which remained occupied for days. By June 19 the parish buildings were once again in church hands, and Archbishop Romero was able to install a new parish team, consisting of a priest and three nuns. Thousands attended the installation Mass and heard the homily from which these selections are taken. The Mass readings were Zechariah 12:10-11; Galatians 3:26-29; Luke 9:18-24.

We will be faithful and firm in defending our rights—
    but with a great love in our hearts,
    because when we defend ourselves with love
    we are seeking the conversion of sinners.
    That is the Christian's vengeance.

                          June 19, 1977

· · ·

As Christians formed in the gospel,
you have the right to organize,
to make concrete decisions inspired by the gospel.
But be very careful not to betray
those evangelical, Christian, supernatural convictions
in the company of those who seek other liberations
that can be merely economic, temporal, political.
Even though working for liberation
along with those who hold other ideologies,
Christians must cling to their original liberation.

                          June 19, 1977

I speak a word of encouragement,
for the Lord's light will always brighten these ways.
New shepherds will come,
but always the same gospel.

June 19, 1977

. . .

We must learn this invitation of Christ:
Those who wish to come after me must renounce
themselves.
Let them renounce themselves,
renounce their comforts,
renounce their personal opinions,
and follow only the mind of Christ,
which can lead us to death
but will surely also lead us to resurrection.

June 19, 1977

The Christian must work to exclude sin
and establish God's reign.
To struggle for this is not Communism.
To struggle for this is not to mix in politics.
It is simply that the gospel demands of today's Christian
more commitment to history.

July 16, 1977

. . .

Pius XII said that the world must be saved from savagery
to make it more human
and thence to make it divine.
That is, all practices that disagree with the gospel
must be removed
if we are to save people.
We must save not the soul at the hour of death
but the person living in history.

July 16, 1977

Not just purgatory but hell awaits
those who could have done good and did not do it.
It is the reverse
of the beatitude that the Bible has
for those who are saved,
for the saints,
who could have done wrong and did not.
Of those who are condemned it will be said:
They could have done good and did not.

July 16, 1977

. . .

When we preach the Lord's word,
we denounce not only the injustices of the social order.
We denounce every sin that is night, that is darkness:
drunkenness, gluttony, lust, adultery, abortion,
all that is the reign of iniquity and sin.
Let them all disappear from our society.

November 27, 1977

We cannot segregate God's word
from the historical reality
in which it is proclaimed.
That would not be God's word.
The Bible would be just a pious history book
in our library.
It is God's word
because it enlightens, contrasts,
repudiates, praises
what is going on today in this society.
November 27, 1977

. . .

The violence we preach is not the violence of the sword,
the violence of hatred.
It is the violence of love,
of brotherhood,
the violence that wills to beat weapons
into sickles for work.
November 27, 1977

Brothers and sisters,
at this moment Christ the redeemer
needs human suffering,
needs the pain of those holy mothers who suffer,
needs the anguish of prisoners who suffer tortures.
Blessed are those who are chosen to continue on earth
the great injustice suffered by Christ,
who keeps on saving the world.
Let us turn that injustice into redemption.

December 1, 1977

Note: Archbishop Romero preached at a Mass for the mothers and other family members of persons who had disappeared while in the custody of government security forces.

. . .

I assure you
that today the holy suffering of so many homes
that suffer unjust orphanhood
is also a suffering that nourishes,
that injects life, love of God,
into this church that is preaching hope,
preaching that we must not despair,
that days of justice must come,
days in which God will triumph over human evil,
over diabolical human wickedness.

December 1, 1977

Do not let the serpent of rancor nest in your hearts.

There is no greater misfortune than a vindictive heart,
even though it be turned against those who have tortured
    your children,
against the criminal hands that have placed them among
    the missing.

Do not hate.

December 1, 1977

. . .

Brothers and sisters, the church is not mistaken.
The church awaits with certainty the hour of redemption.
Those who have disappeared will reappear.
The sorrows of these mothers will be turned into Easter.
The affliction of this aimless people
will become Easter joy
if we join ourselves to Christ
and hope in him.

December 1, 1977

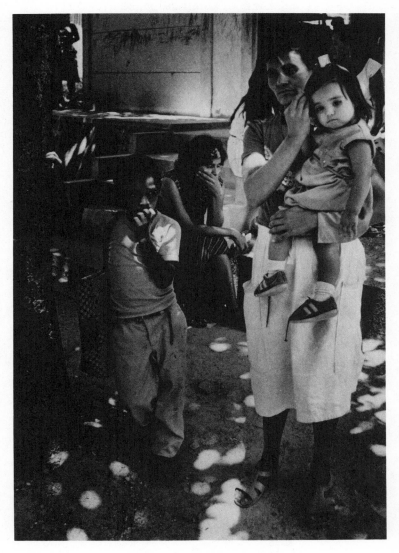

"The church awaits with certainty the hour of redemption. . . . The sorrows of these mothers will be turned into Easter."

Even when all despaired
at the hour when Christ was dying on the cross,
Mary, serene,
awaited the hour of the resurrection.
Mary is the symbol
of the people that suffer oppression and injustice.
Theirs is the calm suffering
that awaits the resurrection.
It is Christian suffering,
the suffering of the church,
which does not accept the present injustices
but awaits without rancor the moment
when the risen one will return
to give us the redemption we await.

December 1, 1977

. . .

A religion of Sunday Mass but of unjust weeks
does not please the Lord.
A religion of much praying
but with hypocrisy in the heart
is not Christian.
A church that sets itself up only to be well off,
to have a lot of money and comfort,
but that forgets to protest injustices,
would not be the true church of our divine redeemer.

December 4, 1977

How arid we human beings are
when the Holy Spirit is not in us!
How cruel people become
when animated not by God's Spirit
but by the spirit of getting ahead in the world!
It pains my heart deeply
to know how our people are tortured,
how the rights of God's image are trampled.
That should not be.
Without God, humans are wild beasts.
Without God, they are deserts.
Their hearts have no blossoms of love.
They are only the perverse persecutors of their brothers
　　and sisters.
That is why there are hearts
capable of betraying others,
of informing on them, not caring
that they are led away to be tortured and killed.

December 5, 1977

Note: Archbishop Romero preached this homily at a Mass at which he administered the sacrament of confirmation in the town of Citalá.

To be a Christian now means to have the courage
to preach the true teaching of Christ
and not to be afraid, not to be silent out of fear
and preach something easy that won't cause problems.
To be a Christian in this hour means to have the courage
that the Holy Spirit gives in his sacrament of
     confirmation
to be valiant soldiers of Christ the King,
to make his teaching prevail,
to reach hearts and proclaim to them the courage
that one must have to defend God's law.

December 5, 1977

. . .

Beginning with me, the bishop,
may this morning be for us a renewal of the Holy Spirit,
of the courage that we must have as Christians.
And, if necessary, may confirmation
become for us a sacrament of martyrdom.
May we too be ready to give our lives for Christ
and not betray him with the cowardice
of today's false Christians.

December 5, 1977

This is why the church has great conflicts:
It denounces sin.
It says to the rich:
Do not sin by misusing your money.
It says to the powerful:
Do not misuse your political influence.
Do not misuse your weaponry.
Do not misuse your power.
It says to sinful torturers:
Do not torture.
You are sinning.
You are doing wrong.
You are establishing the reign of hell on earth.

December 8, 1977

Note: Archbishop Romero preached on sin on the feast of the Immaculate Conception of Mary at the parish of the same name in the town of La Libertad. The doctrine of the immaculate conception states that Mary was free of all sin from the moment she was conceived.

It is very easy to be servants of the word without disturbing the world: a very spiritualistic word, a word without any commitment to history, a word that can sound in any part of the world because it belongs to no part of the world. A word like that creates no problems, starts no conflicts.

What starts conflicts and persecutions, what marks the genuine church, is when the word, burning like the word of the prophets, proclaims to the people and denounces: proclaims God's wonders to be believed and venerated, and denounces the sins of those who oppose God's reign, so that they may tear those sins out of their hearts, out of their societies, out of their laws—out of the structures that oppress, that imprison, that violate the rights of God and of humanity.

This is the hard service of the word.

But God's spirit goes with the prophet, with the preacher, for he is Christ, who keeps on proclaiming his reign to the people of all times.

December 10, 1977

Note: The archbishop preached this homily at the ordination of two priests.

. . .

Israel's history is a theocratic history. God writes it with his prophets, with his human beings, with his deeds. The deeds, Israel's historical events, have a prophetic meaning: What God does with Israel, he wants to do with all peoples. Other peoples must learn from the Bible, from sacred history. It is the paradigm of all histories.

December 11, 1977

A nation is built upon God's designs, and my country's true vocation is to be a land of salvation. The true vocation of Salvadorans is that we should one day become God's kingdom, not just baptized in name but actually Christians, committed to make of our homes, our estates, our farms, our roads, our laws, a structure of salvation, where Salvadorans may feel themselves truly realized as Christians, able to adore their God with freedom, complete freedom, able to proclaim the integral religion that God bids them proclaim, to meet together to reflect on his word without fear of surveillance or evil reports, to love God while meeting in their chapels without being suspected of doing something else. This is the freedom the church preaches.

December 11, 1977

. . .

This is the church's task in each country's history:
to make of each country's individual history
   a history of salvation.

December 11, 1977

What beautiful coffee groves,
what fine cane and cotton fields,
what wonderful farms and lands God has given us!
Nature is so beautiful!
But we see it groan
under oppression, under wickedness, under injustice,
    under abuse,
and the church feels its pain.
Nature looks for a liberation
that will not be mere material well-being
but God's act of power.
God will free nature from sinful human hands,
and along with the redeemed it will sing a hymn of joy
in the liberation God has brought.

December 11, 1977

. . .

Mary and the church in Latin America are marked by poverty.
Vatican Council II says that Mary stands out among the poor
who await redemption from God. Mary appears in the Bible
as the expression of poverty, of humility, of one who needs
everything from God. When she comes to America, her
intimate, motherly conversation is with an Indian, an outcast,
a poor man. Mary's dialog in America begins with a gesture
of poverty.

December 12, 1977

Note: December 12 is the feast of Our Lady of Guadalupe, patroness of
Latin America. In 1531, an Indian, Juan Diego, reported that Mary had
appeared to him and left her image on his cloak, which is now venerated in
the Guadalupe basilica in Mexico City. Archbishop Romero preached this
homily in the church of Our Lady of Guadalupe in San Salvador.

Poverty is freedom.
Poverty is needing others,
needing brothers and sisters,
supporting one another so as to help one another.
This is what Mary is
and this is what the church is in Latin America.

December 12, 1977

. . .

Who knows if the one whose hands are bloodstained
with Father Grande's murder,
or the one who shot Father Navarro,
if those who have killed, who have tortured,
who have done so much evil, are listening to me?
Listen, there in your criminal hideout,
perhaps already repentant,
you too are called to forgiveness.

December 18, 1977

Note: Death squads murdered Father Rutilio Grande, S.J., on March 12, 1977, and Father Alfonso Navarro on May 11, 1977.

When we struggle for human rights, for freedom, for
     dignity,
when we feel that it is a ministry of the church
to concern itself for those who are hungry,
for those who have no schools,
for those who are deprived,
we are not departing from God's promise.
He comes to free us from sin,
and the church knows that sin's consequences
are all such injustices and abuses.
The church knows it is saving the world
when it undertakes to speak also of such things.

December 18, 1977

. . .

It is not an advantage of great value to be well off on this earth
by betraying Christ and his church. It is an advantage that is
very cheap, one that is to be left behind with this life. It is
terrible to hear from the lips of Christ: "Depart from me,
accursed ones, wicked ones; I do not know you, I will be
ashamed of whoever is ashamed of me."

December 19, 1977

With Christ, God has injected himself into history. With the birth of Christ, God's reign is now inaugurated in human time. On this night, as we Christians have done every year for twenty centuries, we recall that God's reign is now in this world and that Christ has inaugurated the fullness of time. His birth attests that God is now marching with us in history, that we do not go alone, and that our aspiration for peace, for justice, for a reign of divine law, for something holy, is far from earth's realities. We can hope for it, not because we humans are able to construct that realm of happiness which God's holy words proclaim, but because the builder of a reign of justice, of love, and of peace is already in the midst of us.

December 25, 1977

. . .

Let us not be disheartened,
even when the horizon of history grows dim and closes
    in,
as though human realities made impossible
the accomplishment of God's plans.
God makes use even of our errors, even of our sins,
so as to make rise over the darkness what Isaiah spoke
    of.
One day prophets will sing not only the return from
    Babylon
but our full liberation.
"The people that walked in darkness have seen a great
    light.
They walk in lands of shadows, but a light has shone
    forth" (Isaiah 9:1-2).

December 25, 1977

For the church, abuses of human life, liberty, and dignity
are a heartfelt suffering.
The church, entrusted with the earth's glory,
believes that in each person is the creator's image
and that everyone who tramples it offends God. . . .
The church takes as spittle in its face,
                as lashes on its back,
                as the cross in its passion,
all that human beings suffer,
even though they be unbelievers. They suffer as God's
        images.
There is no dichotomy between man and God's image.
Whoever tortures a human being,
whoever abuses a human being, whoever outrages a
        human being,
abuses God's image, and the church takes as its own
that cross, that martyrdom.

December 31, 1977

"Whoever outrages a human being abuses God's image. . . ."

A serious examination of living the gospel
is being made among Protestants.
There is conflict—God be blessed.
When a sore spot is touched,
    there is conflict, there is pain.
And Protestantism is putting its hand on the sore spot.
It is saying that one cannot be a true Protestant,
    a true follower of the gospel,
if one does not draw from the gospel
    all the conclusions it contains for this earth.
One cannot live a gospel that is too angelical,
                a gospel of compliance,
                a gospel that is not dynamic peace,
                a gospel that is not of demanding
                        dimensions
in regard to temporal matters also.

                                    December 31, 1977

1978

As the magi from the East followed their star and
    found Jesus,
who filled their hearts with boundless joy,
let us too, even in hours of uncertainty, of shadows, of
    darkness
like those the magi had, not fail to follow that star,
the star of our faith.

January 8, 1978

Note: The feast of the Epiphany (or Manifestation) of Christ was cele-
brated on this day. Readings: Isaiah 60:1-6; Ephesians 3:2-3,5-6; Matthew
2:1-12.

Peace is not the product of terror or fear.
Peace is not the silence of cemeteries.
Peace is not the silent result of violent repression.
Peace is the generous, tranquil contribution of all
    to the good of all.
Peace is dynamism. Peace is generosity.
It is right and it is duty. In it each one feels at home
in this beautiful family that the Epiphany brightens
    with God's light.

January 8, 1978

. . .

The gospel is the great defender and proclaimer of all fundamental rights. The equality rooted in the gospel will not disappear even when political expediencies change. Let us suppose that tomorrow it is no longer expedient for the United States to defend human rights in El Salvador. In that case, the policy would pass away. But the gospel will not pass away. It will always cry out for human freedom and human dignity, even in the worst conditions of persecution.

January 8, 1978

I ask the faithful people who listen to me with love and devotion to pardon me for saying this, but it gives me more pleasure that my enemies listen to me. I know that the reason they listen to me is that I bear them a message of love. I don't hate them. I don't want revenge. I wish them no harm. I beg them to be converted, to come to be happy with the happiness that you faithful ones have.

January 15, 1978

God wants to save us in a people. He does not want to save us in isolation. And so today's church more than ever is accentuating the idea of being a people.

The church therefore experiences conflicts, because it does not want a mass; it wants a people. A mass is a heap of persons, the drowsier the better, the more compliant the better.

The church rejects Communism's slander that it is the opium of the people. It has no intention of being the people's opium. Those that create drowsy masses are others.

The church wants to rouse men and women to the true meaning of being a people. A people is a community of persons where all cooperate for the common good.

January 15, 1978

Note: During the previous week, the Salvadoran press was filled with attacks on Robert Drinan, S.J., member of the U.S. Congress, who had visited El Salvador and spoken bluntly about human rights, and with reports of a forthcoming visit of the Inter-American Human Rights Commission. Archbishop Romero denounced the press coverage as distorted and one-sided and defended the church's role in defending human rights. "The church," he said, "does not want to be one more voice amid the din of distortion and confusion and news management. It wants to be the voice of those who have no voice." The Sunday Mass commemorated the baptism of Christ. The archbishop drew much of his homily from the first reading, taken from the first servant song of Isaiah. Readings: Isaiah 42:1-4,6-7; Acts 10:34-38; Matthew 3:13-17.

A society's reason for existing is not the security of the
        state
but the human being.
Christ said, "Man is not for the sabbath;
the sabbath is for man" (Mark 2:27).
He puts human beings as the objective of all laws and all
        institutions.
People are not for the state; the state is for them.

January 15, 1978

. . .

This is the mission entrusted to the church,
    a hard mission:
to uproot sins from history,
to uproot sins from the political order,
to uproot sins from the economy,
to uproot sins wherever they are.
    What a hard task!
It has to meet conflicts amid so much selfishness,
so much pride,
so much vanity,
so many who have enthroned the reign of sin among us.

January 15, 1978

The church must suffer for speaking the truth,
   for denouncing sin,
   for uprooting sin.
No one wants to have a sore spot touched,
and therefore society twitches
when someone has the courage to touch it
and say: "You have to treat that.
   You have to get rid of that.
   Believe in Christ.
   Be converted."

January 15, 1978

. . .

The day when all of us Salvadorans escape
from that heap of less-human conditions
and as persons and nation
live in more-human conditions,
 not only of merely economic development
but of the kind that lifts us up to faith,
to adoration of only one God,
that day will know our people's real development.

January 15, 1978

We respect the temporal power,
but we do want to create in the people's consciousness
a feeling of being a people, not a mass.
We seek the development of individuals
and a well-being that violates no one's rights
but consists of love and faith between persons,
between sons and daughters of the Father of all.

January 15, 1978

In general, education in our Latin American countries is directed toward the desire to have more, whereas today's youth demand rather to be more, by realizing themselves through service and love.

Let us not develop an education that creates in the mind of the student a hope of becoming rich and having the power to dominate. That does not correspond to the time we live in.

Let us form in the heart of the child and the young person the lofty ideal of loving, of preparing oneself to serve and to give oneself to others.

Anything else would be education for selfishness, and we want to escape the selfishness that is precisely the cause of the great malaise of our societies.

January 22, 1978

Note: The beginning of the school year in El Salvador was the occasion of Archbishop Romero's remarks about education. The readings were Isaiah 9:1-4; 1 Corinthians 1:10-13,17; Matthew 4:12-23.

The church must propose an education that makes people agents of their own development, protagonists of history, not a passive, compliant mass, but human beings able to display their intelligence, their creativity, their desire for the common service of the nation. Education must recognize that the development of the individual and of peoples is the advancement of each and all from less-human to more-human conditions. Persons being educated must find in education a view of development as something in which they must be involved. They must not expect everything to be done for them but must lead the way, each one contributing to the transformation of Latin America.

January 22, 1978

When Christ appeared in Zebulun and Naphtali
   curing the sick,
   raising the dead,
   preaching to the poor,
   bringing hope to the peoples,
something began on earth like when a stone is cast
   into a quiet lake and starts ripples
that finally reach the farthest shores.
Christ appeared in Zebulun and Naphtali
   with the signs of liberation:
      shaking off oppressive yokes,
      bringing joy to hearts,
      sowing hope.
And this is what God is doing now in history.

January 22, 1978

A preaching that awakens,
a preaching that enlightens,
   as when a light turned on
   awakens and annoys a sleeper—
that is the preaching of Christ, calling:
      Wake up! Be converted!
That is the church's authentic preaching.
Naturally, such preaching must meet conflict,
   must spoil what is miscalled prestige,
   must disturb,
   must be persecuted.
It cannot get along with the powers of darkness and sin.

                              January 22, 1978

                   .   .   .

The world does not say, Blessed are the poor.

   The world says, Blessed are the rich. You are worth as much as you have.

   But Christ says, Wrong. Blessed are the poor, for theirs is the kingdom of heaven, because they do not put their trust in what is so transitory.

                              January 29, 1978

Note: Sunday readings: Zephaniah 2:3; 3:12-13; 1 Corinthians 2:26-31; Matthew 5:1-12.

The beatitudes are not something we can understand fully, and that is why there are young people especially who think that the love of the beatitudes is not going to bring about a better world and who opt for violence, for guerrilla war, for revolution. The church will never make that its path. Let it be clear, I repeat, that the church does not choose those ways of violence and that whatever is said to that effect is slander. The church's option is for what Christ says in the beatitudes.

I am not surprised, though, that this is not understood. Young people especially are impatient and want a better world now. But Christ, who preached this message twenty centuries ago, knew that he was sowing a long-term moral revolution in which we human beings come to change ourselves from worldly thinking.

January 29, 1978

. . .

There is one rule by which to judge if God is with us
    or is far away—
the rule that God's word is giving us today:
everyone concerned for the hungry, the naked, the poor,
                for those who have vanished in
                      police custody,
                for the tortured,
                for prisoners,
                for all flesh that suffers,
has God close at hand.

February 5, 1978

Note: Sunday readings: Isaiah 58:7-10; 1 Corinthians 2:1-5; Matthew 5:13-16.

The guarantee of one's prayer is not in saying a lot of
    words.
The guarantee of one's petition is very easy to know:
  How do I treat the poor?
      —because that is where God is.
The degree to which you approach them,
and the love with which you approach them,
or the scorn with which you approach them—
    that is how you approach your God.
What you do to them, you do to God.
The way you look at them is the way you look at God.
February 5, 1978

. . .

God knows how hard it was for me to become
    archbishop.
How timid I have felt before you,
except for the support that you,
    as church, have given me.
You have made your bishop a sign of Christianity.
February 5, 1978

I wish to show that the nucleus of my life is to witness the love of God to humans and of humans among themselves, and that we must show this love through our own lives as Christians and through our conduct. Our lives must witness fidelity to Jesus Christ, poverty and detachment from material goods, and freedom in the face of the powers of the world. That is, our lives must be holy.

But how hard it becomes when one wants to apply the unequivocal teaching of the church to our particular circumstances and put into practice the explicit desires of the Holy Father! No true Catholic can fail to accept this teaching theoretically. But to put it into practice in real life is not so easy or acceptable as it is to remain on the plane of theory.

However, if the *Wall Street Journal* even accused Pope Paul VI of "warmed over Marxism" for his encyclical *Populorum Progressio,* I cannot be surprised if I am accused of the same when I try to be faithful to the Holy Father by applying his words to El Salvador.

From a letter to Cardinal Sebastiano Baggio,
prefect of the Congregation for the Bishops
May 21, 1978

I have tried to follow the supreme shepherd, Jesus Christ,
who directed his love to all but in different ways:
to those dehumanized by anxiety for gain
he showed clearly, out of love, the way to recover
their lost human dignity;
with the poor,
dehumanized outcasts,
he sat at table, also out of love,
to give them hope again.

From a letter to Cardinal Sebastiano Baggio
May 21, 1978

. . .

There are some who desire that I not preach in the manner which I believe the church demands of me. They say I would avoid problems. They affirm that I would not be criticized or accused, that the unity of the bishops would be kept, and that the relations of the church with the government would be smoother. I believe, however, that the voices I should listen to are those of the church in its authentic documents, those of my clergy, largely united around the application that I make of the documents to the conditions of El Salvador, and that of my conscience— not to other voices that do not seem to me so much in agreement with the gospel or the church's teaching.

In order to avoid attacks and slanders from one sector, then, it would seem more opportune to listen to the voices that invite me to change course. God knows what it costs me not to listen to them. But my duty as pastor leads me to remain faithful, in spite of any contradiction.

From a letter to Cardinal Sebastiano Baggio
May 21, 1978

I liked very much the remark of a person who said that this cathedral Mass and my words as teacher in the faith are a veritable university and that many are learning their religion not only intellectually but in a living way.

The liturgy is not just intellectual belief but, before all, a life.

December 3, 1978

. . .

Everyone who struggles for justice,
everyone who makes just claims in unjust surroundings,
is working for God's reign,
even though not a Christian.
The church does not comprise all of God's reign;
God's reign goes beyond the church's boundaries.

The church values everything that is in tune
with its struggle to set up God's reign.
A church that tries only to preserve itself
    pure and uncontaminated
would not be a church of service to people.
The authentic church is one that does not mind
    conversing with prostitutes and publicans and sinners,
    as Christ did—
and with Marxists and those of various political
        movements—
in order to bring them salvation's true message.

December 3, 1978

Some want to keep a gospel so disembodied
    that it doesn't get involved at all
        in the world it must save.
Christ is now in history.
Christ is in the womb of the people.
Christ is now bringing about
    the new heavens and the new earth.

December 3, 1978

. . .

Christ became a man of his people and of his time:
    He lived as a Jew,
    he worked as a laborer of Nazareth,
    and since then he continues to become incarnate in
        everyone.
If many have distanced themselves from the church,
    it is precisely because the church has somewhat
        estranged itself from humanity.
But a church that can feel as its own all that is human
    and wants to incarnate the pain,
    the hope,
    the affliction of all who suffer and feel joy,
such a church will be Christ loved and awaited,
    Christ present.
And that depends on us.

December 3, 1978

When we speak of the church of the poor,
we are not using Marxist dialectic,
as though there were another church of the rich.
What we are saying is that Christ,
inspired by the Spirit of God,
declared, "The Lord has sent me
to preach good news to the poor" (Luke 4:18).

December 3, 1978

. . .

The Christian knows that Christ has been working
    in humanity for twenty centuries
and that the person that is converted to Christ
    is the new human being that society needs
to organize a world
    according to God's heart.

December 3, 1978

Advent should admonish us to discover
in each brother or sister that we greet,
in each friend whose hand we shake,
in each beggar who asks for bread,
in each worker who wants to use the right to join a
    union,
in each peasant who looks for work in the coffee groves,
    the face of Christ.
Then it would not be possible to rob them,
to cheat them,
to deny them their rights.
    They are Christ,
and whatever is done to them
Christ will take as done to him.
This is what Advent is: Christ living among us.

December 3, 1978

Who will put a prophet's eloquence in my words
to shake from their inertia
all those who kneel before the riches of the earth—
those who would like gold, money, lands, power, political
    life
to be their untouchable gods?
    All that is going to end.
There will remain only the satisfaction of having been,
    in regard to money or political life,
    a person faithful to God's will.
One must learn to manage the relative and transitory
    things of earth according to his will,
    not make them absolutes.
There is only one absolute:
he who awaits us in the heaven that will not pass away.

December 10, 1978

The "flesh" is the concrete person. The flesh is we who are present here—people in whom the mark of time can be seen: the child just beginning to live, the vigorous adolescent, the old man nearing the end. The flesh is marked by time. The flesh is the actual human situation, human beings in sin, human beings in painful situations, the people of a nation that seems to have got into a blind alley. The flesh is all of us who live incarnate. The flesh, this frail flesh, this flesh that has beginning and end, that sickens and dies, that sins, that becomes miserable or happy according to whether it obeys God—that is what the Word became. The Word became flesh.

December 17, 1978

Note: Third Sunday of Advent. Readings: Isaiah 61:1-2,10-11; 1 Thessalonians 5:16-24; John 1:6-8,19-28.

The child that we are going to adore at Bethlehem
    is flesh—frail child's flesh.
But in that frail flesh, as though wrapped up,
    is a great gift.
        The Word became flesh!
The most beautiful aspect of Christ is not that he is flesh,
    but without flesh there is no Christ—
flesh that readily makes its own all that is our flesh:
    like us in everything but sin, says St. Paul.

December 17, 1978

I invite you in this hour,
    when El Salvador seems to have no place for joy,
to listen to St. Paul tell us:
    "Be always joyful.
    Be constant in prayer.
    In every circumstance give thanks.
    This is God's will for you in Christ Jesus."
The Christian, the Christian community, must not despair.
If someone dies in the family,
    we must not weep like people without hope.
If the skies have darkened in our nation's history,
    let us not lose hope.
We are a community of hope,
and like the Israelites in Babylon,
    let us hope for the hour of liberation.
It will come.
    It will come because "God is faithful," says St. Paul.
This joy must be like a prayer.
    He who called you is faithful and will keep his
        promises.

December 17, 1978

I know that God's Spirit, who made Christ's body in Mary's womb and keeps making the church in history here in the archdiocese, is a Spirit that is hovering—in the words of Genesis—over a new creation.

I sense that there is something new in the archdiocese.

I am a man, frail and limited, and I do not know what is happening, but I do know that God knows.

My role as pastor is what St. Paul tells me today: "Do not quench the Spirit."

If I say in an authoritarian way to a priest: "Don't do that!" or to a community: "Don't go that way!" and try to set myself up as if I were the Holy Spirit and set about making a church to my liking, I would be quenching the Spirit.

But St. Paul also tells me: "Test everything and keep what is good."

I pray very much to the Holy Spirit for that: the gift of discernment.

December 17, 1978

If Christ had become incarnate now
    and were a thirty-year-old man today,
he could be here in the cathedral
    and we wouldn't know him from the rest of you—
a thirty-year-old man, a peasant from Nazareth,
    here in the cathedral like any peasant
    from our countryside.
The Son of God made flesh would be here
    and we wouldn't know him—
        one completely like us.

December 17, 1978

. . .

How shameful to think that perhaps pagans,
    people with no faith in Christ,
may be better than we
    and nearer to God's reign.

December 17, 1978

. . .

The Bible has a very meaningful expression:
    The Spirit makes all things new.
We are those who grow old,
    and we want everything done to our aged standards.
The Spirit is never old;
    the Spirit is always young.

December 17, 1978

This is the Christian's joy:
 I know that I am a thought in God,
 no matter how insignificant I may be—
 the most abandoned of beings,
 one no one thinks of.
Today, when we think of Christmas giving,
 how many outcasts there are that no one thinks of!
Think to yourselves, you that are outcasts,
 you that feel you are nothing in history:
  "I know that I am a thought in God."

Would that my voice might reach the imprisoned
 like a ray of light, of Christmas hope,
might say also to you,
 the sick,
 the aged,
 the hospital patients,
 you that live in shacks and shantytowns,
 you coffee harvesters trying to garner your only wage
  for the whole year,
 you that are tortured:
God's eternal purpose has thought of all of you.
He loves you,
and, like Mary, he incarnates that thought in his womb.
December 24, 1978

Vatican Council II says: "The mystery of man can now
      be explained only in the mystery of God who
      became man" (*Gaudium et Spes*, 22).
If people want to look into their own mystery—
      the meaning of their pain,
                        of their work,
                        of their suffering,
                        of their hope—
let them put themselves next to Christ.
If they accomplish what Christ accomplished—
      doing the Father's will,
      filling themselves with the life
            that Christ gives the world—
they are fulfilling themselves as true human beings.
If I find, on comparing myself with Christ,
      that my life is the antithesis, the opposite, of his,
my life is a disaster.
I cannot explain that mystery except by returning to
      Christ,
      who gives authentic features
      to a person who wants to be genuinely human.

December 24, 1978

No one can celebrate a genuine Christmas
   without being truly poor.
The self-sufficient,
the proud,
those who, because they have everything, look down on
     others,
those who have no need even of God—
   for them there will be no Christmas.
Only the poor,
the hungry,
those who need someone to come on their behalf,
   will have that someone.
That someone is God,
          Emmanuel,
          God-with-us.
Without poverty of spirit
   there can be no abundance of God.

December 24, 1978

"No one can celebrate a genuine Christmas without being truly poor."

When the poor have nowhere to rest their bodies,
   and their children fleeing from the cold
   find only hammocks strung up in the fields and coffee
      groves,
we must recall that the Savior's good news is for all.
The happiness of the Lord who created us to fulfill his
   salvation is for everyone.

December 24, 1978

. . .

Along with you, my dear brothers and sisters, I too need to receive the good tidings tonight. As shepherd I must announce it, but as shepherd I must also be one of those shepherds of Bethlehem and receive from the angels the news that stirs our hearts. Let us receive it, you and I, with the same simplicity and humility as those shepherds did. The more simple and humble, the more poor and detached from ourselves, the more full of troubles and problems we are, the more bewildering life's ways, the more we must look up to the skies and hear the great news: "A savior is born to you." And let us hear in chorus to that great news, sung throughout the universe, "Glory to God in the heavens, and on earth peace to those whom God loves" (Luke 2:11,14).

December 25, 1978

Through the church's eyes I see the great deficiencies
   in our Christianity that Medellín has now defined for
      us:
   superstitions,
   traditionalism,
   scandals taken because of the truth the church
      preaches.
And those who have money even publish those scandals
   as though they were defending genuine values.
They don't realize they are defending the indefensible:
   a lie, a falsehood, a lifeless traditionalism,
   and, much worse, certain economic interests,
which, lamentably, the church served.
But that was a sin of the church,
   deceiving and not telling the truth
      when it should have.

December 31, 1978

Note: Feast of the Holy Family. Archbishop Romero is referring to the 1968 general conference of Latin American bishops at Medellín, Colombia, which said: "We know that many families in Latin America have been incapable of educating in the faith, either because they are unstable or have disintegrated, and because they have imparted this education in purely traditional terms, at times with mythical and superstitious aspects. From this situation springs the necessity of bestowing on today's families the elements which will rebuild their evangelizing capacity in accordance with the doctrine of the church" (*The Church in the Present-day Transformation of Latin America in the Light of the Council,* Latin American Episcopal Council, Bogotá, Colombia, 1970, official English version, p. 88).

Certain wealthy Salvadorans, accustomed to a church unconcerned with social justice, opposed Archbishop Romero by appealing to supposed Catholic tradition. Radio and newspaper commentators and paid advertisements often attacked him, accusing him of deviating from Catholic teaching and even of supporting Communism and terrorism, because of his support of the rights of the poor. He alludes here to those attacks.

There are families where the faith is not developed
because what is given is a tradition
    poisoned by economic and political interests and
    wrapped up with things of faith.
They want a religion that will merely support those
       interests.
And when the church protests against
    such selfishness, sins, and abuses,
    then it is thought to be departing from the truth,
and these Christians, with their children and all,
    go away and continue to live a tradition
    that is not the true Christian tradition.

December 31, 1978

. . .

Those who reject me
    do me a great honor,
because I somewhat resemble Jesus Christ,
    who was also a stumbling block.

December 31, 1978

1979

I was told this week that I should be careful,
that something was being plotted against my life.
   I trust in the Lord,
    and I know that the ways of Providence
   protect one who tries to serve him.

January 1, 1979

The pastoral and evangelical teaching of Vatican Council II, which in 1968 became also the pastoral policy for Latin America, proclaimed a total salvation, and it continues to raise questions for us now at the dawn of a new Medellín to take place at Puebla. This teaching declares that the liberation that Christ has brought is of the whole human being. The whole person must be saved: body and soul, individual and society. God's reign must be established now on earth.

That reign of God finds itself hindered, manacled, by many idolatrous misuses of money and power. Those false gods must be overthrown, just as the first evangelizers in the Americas overthrew the false gods that our natives adored. Today the idols are different. They are called money, political interests, and national security. As idolatries, they are trying to displace God from his altar. The church declares that people can only be happy when, like the magi, they adore the one true God.

January 7, 1979

Note: The Latin American bishops' conference that met at Puebla, Mexico, in 1979 was a follow-up to the Medellín conference (see note on page 53).

In the symbolic gifts of incense, gold, and myrrh,
    the wise men bring
the pain, the sorrows, and the concerns of their peoples
    to beg salvation from the only one who can give it.
So it is in our own history.
Each Sunday when I speak of the specific events of the
    week,
    I am only a poor adorer of the Lord telling him:
Lord, I bring you what the people produce,
    what the interaction of these people of El Salvador,
        rich and poor, rulers and ruled, brings forth.
This is what we bring the Lord.

January 7, 1979

. . .

My position as pastor obliges me to solidarity
with everyone who suffers
and to embody in myself every effort for human dignity.

January 7, 1979

Christ says his reign is not of this world.

As Pope Pius XI explained when he decreed the feast of Christ the King, that does not mean that Christ has nothing to do with the power and wealth of earth.

It means that he will use a different basis, a religious basis, to judge the consciences of political leaders and of the rich (and of the poor also), judging them from the eschatological and transcendent perspective of God's reign.

January 14, 1979

. . .

Peoples are free to choose the political system they want
    but not free to do whatever they feel like.
They will have to be judged by God's justice
    in the political or social system they choose.
God is the judge of all social systems.
Neither the gospel nor the church can be monopolized
    by any political or social movement.

January 14, 1979

The present form of the world passes away,
and there remains the joy of having used this world
    to establish God's rule here.
All pomp, all triumphs, all selfish capitalism,
    all the false successes of life will pass
    with the world's form.
All of that passes away.
What does not pass away is love.
When one has turned money, property, work in one's
        calling
    into service of others,
then the joy of sharing
    and of feeling that all are one's family
does not pass away.
In the evening of life you will be judged on love.

January 21, 1979

Note: This is an excerpt from the homily delivered at the funeral Mass of Father Octavio Ortiz and four young men killed by security forces that raided a retreat house where a youth group was gathered for a retreat. A crowd of thousands gathered before the doors of the cathedral for the Mass on Sunday morning. "In the evening of life you will be judged on love" is a paraphrase of Saint John of the Cross.

One can perfectly well be a nuncio or a military chaplain, provided one is converted to the gospel. If these duties are carried out with a genuine sense of being a church that tries first of all to be faithful to the gospel rather than to earthly advantages—not to diplomatic career advancement or advantages obtained from the military—then indeed there can and should be representatives in the midst of the diplomatic and the military worlds. But they must be truly voices of the gospel and of the church. That is where the problem seems to be: conversion to the gospel.

Press conference, Puebla, Mexico
February 9, 1979

Note: Archbishop Romero attended the Latin American bishops' conference at Puebla, Mexico, January 27 to February 13, 1979.

In our preaching to rich and poor, it is not that we pander to the sins of the poor and ignore the virtues of the rich. Both have sins and both need conversion. But the poor, in their condition of need, are disposed to conversion. They are more conscious of their need of God. All of us, if we really want to know the meaning of conversion and of faith and confidence in another, must become poor, or at least make the cause of the poor our own inner motivation. That is when one begins to experience faith and conversion: when one has the heart of the poor, when one knows that financial capital, political influence, and power are worthless, and that without God we are nothing. To feel that need of God is faith and conversion.

February 18, 1979

Note: This is taken from Archbishop Romero's first Sunday homily after returning from the Puebla conference, at which the Latin American bishops expressed the church's "option for the poor."

I cannot change
except to seek to follow the gospel more closely.
And I can quite simply call to everyone:
Let us be converted
so that Christ may look upon our faith
and have mercy on us.

February 18, 1979

.   .   .

Like the prophets' words proclaiming to Babylon's
    captives
times of joy and freedom,
the church's word calling to love, reconciliation, and
    pardon
can seem like a mockery
while others call to violence, kidnapping, and terrorism.
But the church will never walk that path,
    and whatever is said to that effect is false.
It is a slander that only enhances in the church
    the glory of our persecution.

February 18, 1979

I recognize my limitations and my miseries,
but I cannot renounce the role that Christ has given me:
to be the sign of the church's unity, teaching, and truth
in the archdiocese.

February 25, 1979

. . .

I simply want to be the builder of a great affirmation,
the affirmation of God,
who loves us
and who wants to save us.

February 25, 1979

The church renews itself. We cannot preserve old traditions that no longer have any reason for being, much less those structures in which sin has enthroned itself and from which come abuses, injustices, and disorders. We cannot call a society, a government, or a situation Christian when our brothers and sisters suffer so much in those inveterate and unjust structures.

February 25, 1979

. . .

When we speak of the church of the poor,
    we are simply telling the rich also:
Turn your eyes to this church
    and concern yourselves for the poor
        as for yourselves.
At Puebla we said the poor are a concern of Christ,
    who will say at the end of life:
"Whatever you did to one of these poor ones,
    you did to me."

March 4, 1979

You know that the air and water are being polluted, as is everything we touch and live with, and we go on corrupting the nature that we need. We don't realize we have a commitment to God to take care of nature. To cut down a tree, to waste water when there is such a shortage of it, to let buses poison our atmosphere with those noxious fumes, to burn rubbish anywhere—all that concerns our alliance with God.

March 11, 1979

.   .   .

It would be too bad if the same thing were to happen with the Puebla document as with Medellín's: Many Catholics, out of prejudice, at times out of ignorance, did not put it into practice.

If our own archdiocese has become controversial, let there be no doubt in your minds: It is for its desire to be faithful to this new evangelization.

From Vatican Council II until now, and in particular in the meetings of Latin American bishops, the demand is for an evangelization that is committed and fearless.

March 11, 1979

A church that suffers no persecution but enjoys the privileges and support of the things of earth— beware!—is not the true church of Jesus Christ.

March 11, 1979

. . .

I look at you, dear friends, and I know
that my humble ministry is only that of Moses:
    to transmit the word—"Thus says the Lord."
And what pleasure it gives me when you say
    in your intimate hearts,
    or at times in words or in letters I receive,
what the people replied to Moses:
    "We will do all that Yahweh has ordained"
        (Exodus 24:3).

March 18, 1979

Note: Third Sunday of Lent. Readings: Exodus 20:1-17; 1 Corinthians 1:22-25; John 2:13-25.

The other day a priest told me a man wanted to go to confession who hadn't done so for forty years. He said he wanted to be converted, as he had heard about here in the cathedral.

When they say I preach political matters, I refer to these testimonies of conversion to God. That is what I seek: conversion to God. If I point to political affairs here, it is often because of the corruption of political affairs, so that those whom God loves even when they are mired in sin may be converted too.

March 18, 1979

.   .   .

You shall not kill!
When Christ perfected this commandment,
  he said:
When you begin to hate,
  you have also begun to kill.

March 18, 1979

Those who, in the biblical phrase, would save their lives—that is, those who don't want commitments, who don't want to get into problems, who want to stay outside whatever demands our involvement—they will lose their lives.

What a terrible thing to have lived well off, with no suffering, not getting into problems, quite tranquil, quite settled, with good connections— politically, economically, socially—lacking nothing, having everything.

To what good?

They will lose their lives.

"But those who for love of me uproot themselves and accompany the people and go with the poor in their suffering and become incarnate and feel as their own the pain and the abuse—they will secure their lives, because my Father will reward them."

April 1, 1979

Note: Fifth Sunday of Lent. Readings: Jeremiah 31:31-34; Hebrews 5:7-9; John 12:20-33.

To each one of us Christ is saying:
If you want your life and mission to be fruitful like mine,
  do like me.
Be converted into a seed that lets itself be buried.
  Let yourself be killed. Do not be afraid.
Those who shun suffering will remain alone.
  No one is more alone than the selfish.
But if you give your life out of love for others,
  as I give mine for all, you will reap a great harvest.
You will have the deepest satisfactions.
Do not fear death or threats. The Lord goes with you.

April 1, 1979

At this moment, in the name of all my priests,
    I beg pardon
for not having shown all the fortitude the gospel asks
    in serving the people that we must lead,
for having confused them at times,
    softening too much the message of the cross,
which is hard.

April 1, 1979

The church cannot agree with the forces that put their hope only in violence.

The church does not want the liberation it preaches to be confused with liberations that are only political and temporal.

The church does concern itself with earthly liberation—it feels pain for those who suffer, for the illiterate, for those without electricity, without a roof, without a home.

But it knows that human misfortune is found not only there. It is inside, deeper, in the heart—in sin.

While supporting all the people's just claims, the church wants to lift those demands to a higher plane and free people from the chains that are sin, death, and hell.

It wants to tell us to work to be truly free, with a freedom that begins in the heart: the freedom of God's children—the freedom that makes us into God's children by taking from us the chains of sin.

April 8, 1979

Christian love goes beyond all categories of regimes and systems. The church is not identified with any political system. The church cannot identify itself with any political organization. The church cannot be a system.

It is above all systems, because it brings with it the insurmountable power of the paschal mystery—of Christ's death and resurrection.

April 12, 1979

Note: This homily was given on Holy Thursday.

A civilization of love
    that did not demand justice of people
    would not be a true civilization:
    it would not delineate genuine human relations.
It is a caricature of love to try to cover over with alms
    what is lacking in justice,
to patch up with an appearance of benevolence
    when social justice is missing.
True love begins by demanding what is just
    in the relations of those who love.

April 12, 1979

If there is not truth in love, there is hypocrisy.

Often, fine words are said, handshakes given, perhaps even a kiss, but at bottom there is no truth.

A civilization where the trust of one for another is lost, where there is so much lying and no truth, has no foundation of love. There can't be love where there is falsehood.

Our environment lacks truth. And when the truth is spoken, it gives offense, and the voices that speak the truth are put to silence.

April 12, 1979

"My God, my God, why have you forsaken me?"

He is not forsaken, but Christ does feel the pain and anguish that our hearts must sometimes suffer.

It's the psychology of suffering: to feel alone, to feel that no one understands, to feel forsaken. . . .

God is not failing us when we don't feel his presence.

Let's not say: God doesn't do what I pray for so much, and therefore I don't pray any more.

God exists, and he exists even more, the farther you feel from him.

God is closer to you when you think he is farther away and doesn't hear you.

When you feel the anguished desire for God to come near because you don't feel him present, then God is very close to your anguish.

When are we going to understand that God is not only a God who gives happiness but that he tests our faithfulness in moments of affliction?

It is then that prayer and religion have most merit: when one is faithful in spite of not feeling the Lord's presence.

Let us learn from that cry of Christ that God is always our father and never forsakes us, and that we are closer to him than we think.

April 13, 1979

Note: This homily was given on Good Friday.

You that have so much social sensitivity, you that cannot stand this unjust situation in our land: fine—God has given you that sensitivity, and if you have a call to political activism, God be blessed. Develop it.

But look. Don't waste that call; don't waste that political and social sensitivity on earthly hatred, vengeance, and violence.

Lift up your hearts. Look at the things above.

April 15, 1979

Note: Easter Sunday. Readings: Acts 10:34,37- 43; Colossians 3:1-4; John 20:1-9.

"Receive the Holy Spirit."
Christ himself explains: "As my father sent me, I send
    you."
He means that the church is born with this breath of his,
and the mission that the church will bear to the world
    for all time will be that of Christ dead and risen.
The church celebrates its liturgy and preaches its word
    only for this:
        to save from sin,
        to save from slaveries,
        to overthrow idolatries,
        to proclaim the one God who loves us.
That will be the church's difficult mission,
and it knows that in fulfilling that mission,
    which earned for Christ a cross and humiliations,
it will have to be ready also not to betray that message
and, if necessary, to suffer martyrdom like him—
    suffer the cross, humiliation, persecution.

April 22, 1979

Note: Second Sunday of Easter. Readings: Acts 4:32-35; 1 John 5:1-6;
John 20:19-31.

You have to understand clearly that the conflict is between the government and the people. There is conflict with the church because we take the people's side. I insist that the church is not looking for a fight with the government. For my part, I don't want quarrels with the government. When they say I am a subversive and that I meddle in political matters, I say it's not true. I try to define the church's mission, which is a prolongation of Christ's. The church must save the people and be with them in their search for justice. Also, it must not let them follow ways of unjust violence, hatred, and vengeance. In this sense, we accompany the people, a people that suffers greatly. Of course, those that trample the people must be in conflict with the church.

Interview, May 1979,
in *Vida Nueva*,
June 2, 1979

"The church must save the people and be with them in their search for justice."

It is wrong to be sad.
Christians cannot be pessimists.
Christians must always nourish in their hearts
the fullness of joy.
Try it, brothers and sisters;
I have tried it many times and in the darkest moments,
when slander and persecution were at their worst:
to unite myself intimately with Christ, my friend,
and to feel a comfort
that all the joys of the earth do not give—
the joy of feeling oneself close to God,
even when humans do not understand one.
It is the deepest joy the heart can have.

May 20, 1979

Sincerely, I have never favored anyone,
   because I have been committed only to my God.
I have always proclaimed my autonomy
   so as to be able to praise what is good in any human
      being
as well as to be able to rebuke with total freedom
   what is evil and unjust in any human being.
That is what the church is here for.

                                        May 20, 1979

The political circumstances of peoples change,
and the church will not be the toy of varying
conditions.
The church must always be the horizon of God's
love. . . .
Christian love surpasses the categories
of all regimes and systems.
If today it is democracy and tomorrow socialism
and later something else,
that is not the church's concern.
It is your concern, you who are the people,
you who have the right to organize that every people
has.
Organize your social system.
The church will always stay outside, autonomous,
in order to be, in whatever system,
the conscience and the judge of the attitudes
of those who manage those systems or regimes.

May 20, 1979

Transcendence means breaking through encirclements.
It means not letting oneself be imprisoned by matter.
It means saying in one's mind:
    I am above all the things that try to enchain me.
Neither death nor life nor money nor power nor flattery—
    nothing can take from one this transcendent calling.
There is something beyond history.
There is something that passes the threshold
    of matter and time.
There is something called the transcendent,
      the eschatological,
      the beyond,
      the final goal.
God, who does not let things contain him
    but who contains all,
is the goal
    to which the risen Christ calls us.

                May 27, 1979

It's amusing:
This week I received accusations from both extremes—
from the extreme right, that I am a Communist;
from the extreme left, that I am joining the right.
I am not with the right or with the left.
I am trying to be faithful to the word
    that the Lord bids me preach,
    to the message that cannot change,
which tells both sides the good they do
    and the injustices they commit.

June 3, 1979

The church is not an opposition party.
The church is a force of God in the people,
a force of inspiration
so that the people may forge their own destiny.
The church does not want to impose
political or social systems.
It must not. That is not its field of competence.
But the church calls for the freedom of peoples—
for them not to have a single standard imposed on
them,
but for humans to be able to further
through their skills and technology
what the people think they want—
for them to shape their own destiny,
free to choose their own way to achieve the destiny
that God points out to them.

June 10, 1979

When we leave Mass,
we ought to go out
the way Moses descended Mount Sinai:
  with his face shining,
  with his heart brave and strong
    to face the world's difficulties.

June 17, 1979

. . .

It makes me sad to think that some people don't evolve. They
say: "Everything the church does today is wrong, because it
isn't the way we did things as children." They think back to
their school days and long for a static Christianity, one like a
museum that preserves things.

Christianity is not like that, and neither is the gospel. It has
to be the leaven of the present time. It must denounce not the
sins of the times of Moses and Egypt nor the times of Christ
and Pilate and Herod and the Roman Empire, but the sins of
today, here in El Salvador, the ones you must live among in
your surroundings. We must be the seed of holiness and unity
here amid the tremendous things that are going on among our
own people, with whom we are in communion as a church.

June 17, 1979

Life is always sacred.
The Lord's commandment,
Thou shalt not kill,
makes all life sacred.
Blood poured out,
even a sinner's,
always cries out to God.
And those who kill
are always murderers.

June 24, 1979

Note: Feast of the Birth of St. John the Baptist. Father Rafael Palacios had been assassinated on June 20. He was the fifth priest murdered while Oscar Romero was archbishop.

. . .

Let us not put our trust
in earthly liberation movements.
Yes, they are providential,
but only if they do not forget
that all the liberating force in the world
comes from Christ.

June 24, 1979

Death is the sign of sin,
and sin produces it so directly among us:
violence, murder, torture (which leaves so many dead),
hacking with machetes,
throwing into the sea—people discarded!
All this is the reign of hell.

July 1, 1979

. . .

Let it be quite clear
that if we are being asked
to collaborate
with a pseudo peace,
a false order,
based on repression and fear,
we must recall that the only order
and the only peace
that God wants
is one based on truth and justice.
Before these alternatives,
our choice is clear:
We will follow God's order,
not men's.

July 1, 1979

What a beautiful experience it is
to try to follow Christ a bit
and for that to receive the broadside of insults,
of disagreements,
of slanders,
of lost friendships,
of being considered suspect!

July 8, 1979

. . .

If some day they take the radio station away from us,
if they close down our newspaper,
if they don't let us speak,
if they kill all the priests and the bishop too,
and you are left, a people without priests,
each one of you must be God's microphone,
each one of you must be a messenger,
a prophet.
The church will always exist
as long as there is one baptized person.

July 8, 1979

I am glad, brothers and sisters,
that our church is persecuted
precisely for its preferential option for the poor
and for trying to become incarnate
on behalf of the poor.
And I want to say to all the people,
to rulers,
to the rich and powerful:
If you do not become poor,
if you do not concern yourselves
for the poverty of our people
as though they were your own family,
you will not be able to save society.

July 15, 1979

. . .

What good are beautiful highways and airports,
beautiful buildings full of spacious apartments,
if they are only put together
with the blood of the poor,
who are not going to enjoy them?

July 15, 1979

Christ has representatives here and now in the world: us, his church, the community. And so when I focus on the week gone by, I attend to a work that is proper for the church. It should be the principal task of us priests, nuns, and faithful—of all pastoral workers. We are not politicians. We turn the gospel's light onto the political scene, but the main thing for us is to light the lamp of the gospel in our communities.

July 22, 1979

Note: In his Sunday homilies, Archbishop Romero always included an account of events of the week gone by.

.   .   .

I want to repeat to you what I said once before:
the shepherd does not want security
while they give no security to his flock.

July 22, 1979

Christ invokes eternal justice—
not like on this earth, where even though
you petition the president of the supreme court
everything stays the same.
He is not Christ.
But there is a Christ above him, who will demand
an accounting of him
and will demand an accounting of all the accomplices
in this unjust situation in El Salvador.

July 29, 1979

. . .

These homilies try to be this people's voice.
They try to be the voice of those who have no voice.
And so, without doubt, they displease
those who have too much voice.
This poor voice will find echo
in those who love the truth
and who truly love our dear people.

July 29, 1979

Let not the Church's mission
of evangelizing and working for justice
be confused with subversive activities.
It is very different—
unless the gospel is to be called subversive,
because it does indeed touch the foundations
of an order that should not exist,
because it is unjust.

August 5, 1979

The only violence that the gospel admits
is violence to oneself.
When Christ lets himself be killed,
that is violence—letting himself be killed.
Violence to oneself is more effective
than violence against others.
It is very easy to kill,
especially when one has weapons,
but how hard it is
to let oneself be killed for love of the people!
August 12, 1979

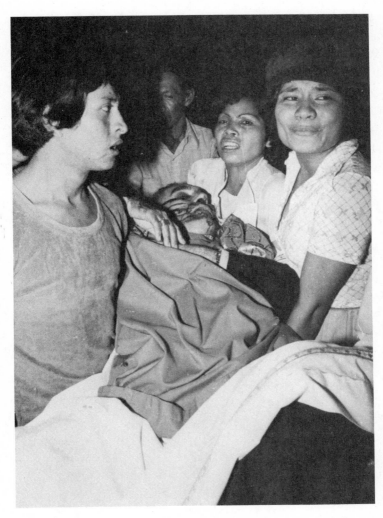

"How hard it is to let oneself be killed for love of the people!"

I denounce, above all, the absolutizing of wealth.
This is the great evil in El Salvador:
wealth, private property,
as an untouchable absolute.
Woe to the one who touches that high-tension wire!
It burns.

August 12, 1979

. . .

How it delights me in humble villages
when the people and the children come crowding around!
You arrive at the town and they come out to meet you.
They come with trust, because they know
that you are bringing them God's message.

August 12, 1979

If I have the joy of possessing heaven,
I would not mind being in that heaven
near to those who today
declare themselves my enemies,
because there we will not be enemies.
I am never anyone's enemy.
But let those who without cause want to be my enemies
be converted to love,
and in love we shall meet in the blessedness of God.

September 2, 1979

Those who do not understand transcendence
cannot understand us.
When we speak of injustice here below
and denounce it,
they think we are playing politics.
It is in the name of God's just reign
that we denounce the injustices of the earth.
                    September 2, 1979

                        .   .   .

    I believe that the bishop
    has much to learn from the people.
    Precisely in those charisms
    that the Holy Spirit gives to the people
the bishop finds the touchstone of his authenticity.
                    September 9, 1979

Anyone who is chosen, for society's need,
to be a cabinet member,
to be president of the republic,
to be archbishop—
to be a servant—
is the servant of God's people.
That must not be forgotten.
The attitude to be taken in these offices is not
"I'm in charge here! What I want must be done."
You are only a human being, God's servant.
You must be at the Lord's beck and call
to serve the people according to God's will
and not according to your whim.

September 23, 1979

I want to assure you—
and I ask your prayers to be faithful to this promise—
that I will not abandon my people
but that together with them I will run all the risks
that my ministry demands.

November 11, 1979

. . .

In the measure in which we are church,
that is, true Christians,
incarnating the gospel,
in that measure we will be the timely citizens,
the Salvadorans needed at this moment.
If we retreat from this inspiration of God's word,
we can be pragmatists,
political opportunists,
but we will not be Christians
who are shapers of history.

November 11, 1979

With this people
it is not hard to be a good shepherd.
They are a people that impel to their service
us who have been called to defend their rights
and to be their voice.

November 18, 1979

We must not seek the child Jesus
in the pretty figures of our Christmas cribs.
We must seek him among the undernourished children
who have gone to bed tonight without eating,
among the poor newsboys
who will sleep covered with newspapers in doorways.
                                    December 24, 1979

"We must seek the child Jesus among the undernourished children, . . . among the poor newsboys. . . ."

1980

I repeat what I told you once before when we feared
we might be left without a radio station:
God's best microphone is Christ,
and Christ's best microphone is the church,
and the church is all of you.
Let each one of you,
in your own job, in your own vocation—
nun, married person, bishop, priest,
high-school or university student,
workman, laborer, market woman—
each one in your own place live the faith intensely
and feel that in your surroundings
you are a true microphone of God our Lord.

January 27, 1980

Yesterday, when a journalist asked me
where I found inspiration
for my work and my preaching, I told him:
"Your question is very timely, for just now
I have come from my retreat.
If it were not for this prayer and reflection
with which I try to keep united with God,
I would be no more
than what St. Paul says:
clanging metal."

March 2, 1980

Nothing is so important to the church as human life,
as the human person,
above all, the person of the poor and the oppressed,
who, besides being human beings,
are also divine beings,
since Jesus said that whatever is done to them
he takes as done to him.
That bloodshed, those deaths,
are beyond all politics.
They touch the very heart of God.

March 16, 1980

This is the fundamental thought of my preaching:
Nothing is so important to me as human life.
Taking life is something so serious, so grave—
more than the violation of any other human right—
because it is the life of God's children,
and because such bloodshed only negates love,
awakens new hatreds,
makes reconciliation and peace impossible.

March 16, 1980

God's program to liberate the people is a transcendent one.

Perhaps I repeat this idea too much, but I will keep on saying it. In wanting to solve immediate problems, we run the great danger of forgetting that immediate solutions can be mere band-aids and not real solutions. A genuine solution must fit into God's program. Whatever solution we may decide on for a better land distribution, a better financial system for the country, a political arrangement better suited for the common good of the citizens, will have to be found in the context of definitive liberation.

March 23, 1980

"God's reign is already present on our earth in mystery.
When the Lord comes, it will be brought to perfection"
        (Gaudium et Spes, 39).
That is the hope that inspires Christians.
We know that every effort to better society,
especially when injustice and sin are so ingrained,
is an effort that God blesses,
                that God wants,
                that God demands of us.

March 24, 1980

Note: This passage is from Archbishop Romero's last homily. He was assassinated as he concluded the homily.